KEITH SKIPPER'S NORFOLK SCRAPBOOK

Further details of Poppyland Publishing titles can be found at
www.poppyland.co.uk
where clicking on the 'Support and Resources' button
will lead to pages specially compiled to support this book

Join us for more Norfolk and Suffolk stories and background at
www.facebook.com/poppylandpublishing

and follow **@poppylandpub**

Love to Gal Margaret
— and mind how yew go!

KEITH SKIPPER'S
Norfolk Scrapbook

Keith Skipper

(Norfolk, 2016 '

POPPYLAND
PUBLISHING

Picture credits:

Front cover: Trevor Allen

Pictures in this publication are from the author's own collection. Where known individual photographers have been credited in the picture caption.

First published 2015 by Poppyland Publishing, Cromer, NR27 9AN
www.poppyland.co.uk

ISBN 978 1 909796 19 5

Designed and typeset in 12 on 14.4 pt Gilgamesh
Printed by Lightning Source

DEDICATION

Heartfelt thanks to all who have shared a love of Norfolk over the years. Family and friends make every chapter special.

Smile — you're on the wireless. Skip in his early days at Radio Norfolk shows what is expected of a home-grown presenter on the Dinnertime Show from Cell 33.

INTRODUCTION

I'm a long-term disciple of the "don't throw that away 'cos it might come in handy one day" creed, so beloved of those reluctant to treat order and tidiness as proper virtues.

The magpie instinct has kept me company throughout my industrious (I could put "illustrious" but that would be boasting) Norfolk career as writer, broadcaster and entertainer. Oh, not forgetting role model for anyone contemplating life as a cussed parochialist.

I spent 17 years as a full-time scribe on our local newspapers, including a number of seasons as Norwich City football correspondent for the Eastern Daily Press and Evening News. So I know what promotion and relegation feel like even if I can't do a three-point turn or drive myself to distraction.

Then followed 15 years on air with BBC Radio Norfolk, most of them spent as host of the Dinnertime Show from a studio I called Cell 33. Remember, dinnertime in Norfolk traditionally takes place around noon and is a fairly informal diversion. Nothing to do with crinkly serviettes, wine glasses and flickering candles surrounding posh people in the evenings.

When that spell of homely incarceration ended in 1995, and I felt no compulsion at all to forsake my native soil, freelance furrows beckoned. Well, I was too young to go straight into the Duntroshin retirement home on the edge of Happisburgh cliffs.

"Freelance" is a clever way of describing an exhausting but exhilarating period of making life up as I jogged along, writing a load more articles and books, calling on talented friends to help me make DVDs and CDs, mardling at countless local events and leading the Press Gang entertainment troupe around local temples of culture, all the time trying to make sense of so many drastic changes imposed on dear old Norfolk.

I have collected enough incriminating evidence over the last 30 years or so to take politicians, planners, developers and other prophets of boom to a public tribunal on top of Beeston Bump to answer serious charges of wilful damage inflicted on one of the last remaining corners of civilisation in this country.

That must wait, however, while I share some of my cherished tucked-away bits and pieces acting as a kind of insulation against so much misguided "progress" since I left school still thinking the Swinging Sixties had more to do with a swishing scythe and sugar-beet hook than any hedonistic pursuits finding favour in the USA (Uther Side of Attleborough).

This volume is my 39th off the production line since writing books became a leading excuse for getting out of the washing-up and other mundane domestic necessities. Naturally, it includes several pertinent reminders of what I will miss most from what is rapidly turning into a glorious Norfolk sunset before a potentially all-enveloping darkness.

I exaggerate slightly, of course, but there can't be much harm in putting the wind up those who believe Norfolk should stop paying homage to the past, even if it was a lot cheaper, and line up meekly alongside those in the fast lane to nowhere in particular.

I thank warmly a big band of enthusiasts from all Norfolk walks of life for topping up my magpie's nest at regular intervals over the years. Old postcards and photographs multiplied by the outing along with cuttings, some yellow with age, vintage local magazines, plus old yarns and jokes ready for fresh daubs of paint.

I include also various posters, programmes and other memorabilia closely connected with invitations to hold forth at all manner of occasions since finding my feet at cricket dinners in the 1960s. It soon became clear I was much more use off the field than on it.

Perhaps my biggest bouquet of gratitude ought to go to my wife Diane and our sons Danny and Robin for goading me into a long-overdue purge in the study and several other rooms into which my mounting collections had overflowed.

I spent weeks sifting and sorting, followed by hours of sighing and saying goodbye to old friends I simply couldn't live without. Sentiment eventually made way for common sense and space I never knew I had.

This permanent home provided by Peter Stibbons at Poppyland Publishing — where it has been known for literary mountains to grow out of paper molehills - proves it is never too late to make order and tidiness your friends.

Even so, I suspect there'll still be time to feed the magpie a few more scattered bits and pieces when it flutters on to my freshly-cleared desk.

KEITH SKIPPER
CROMER   2015

"And if any of you lapse into 'Mummerzet', our Accent Troubleshooter here will gently persuade you back to proper Norfolk."

Reflecting quietly outside Booton's many-pinnacled parish church, near Reepham. It is known as the Cathedral of the Fields.

Creamy waves at Cromer. (Trevor Allen)

CROMER PIER

Waves patrol below
Hands pump above
Slap and clap
Stage tests water
With toes in the sea
Lifeboat stabled just
Beyond the footlights
Does old Blogg
Take a bow
On stormy nights?
End of the pier where
An era lives on
Out of curiosity
And affection
For old-fashioned ways

Heading the queue for another crab treat.
(Trevor Allen)

Old fishermen never die – even if they catch everything

Broads marshman Eric Edwards, a friend of
many years, passes on a few tips to a rather
dubious apprentice.

Briefly lamented . . .

Martha's husband died
and she decided to put
an announcement in the local
paper. She told the girl in the
office she wanted to keep it as
short as possible.

"Jest put 'Horry Grimble
dead'," she suggested.

"Actually, my dear, you can
have up to six words for the
same price," said the girl.

"Would you like to add
anything?"

Martha pondered for a while
and then said: "Right, kin yew
add: 'Ferret for sale'?"

**Old curtain-makers never die — they just pull themselves
together.**

WATER FRONT, STOKESBY

W 132

A spot to soak up the timeless glories of our local waterways. Stokesby, a few miles from Great Yarmouth, still extends a gentle welcome.

The "Pit", West Street, North Creake.

The Pit at North Creake — without a paddle in sight!

In reflective mood at How Hill,
near Ludham, one of my favourite
Norfolk spots.

ALTOGETHER NOW ...

I recall a jolly warm-up jape at one of Great Yarmouth's summer shows in the early 1960s when this sort of seaside entertainment was an integral part of the holiday programme.

Patrons were invited to settle into their seats with a free bingo card. A gleaming new car was the prize. Numbers rang out and excitement mounted ...

Suddenly, the theatre roof was in serious danger of taking off for a dip in the sea as players jumped to their feet and roared "HOUSE!" Gradually, it dawned on them that the game had been fixed to ensure everybody got to the winning line at the same time.

A delicious spoof to create the right sort of mood for holiday fun and laughter in what now appears to be a more tolerant and amiable era. Such an exercise these days, methinks, could well result in vandalism, riots and a few hundred threats to sue.

Entertainment bosses were prepared to risk taking customers for a ride, forcing them to laugh at their own embarrassing folly — the joke was based on greed after all — and even the promise not to tell others planning to see the show.

A bit before my time as trams add to the colour and bustle of Great Yarmouth
Market Place.

A full house at the Wellington Pier Gardens in Great Yarmouth to hear music
from what looks like a giant birdcage in the middle.

Mundesley Festival stalwart Phil Drackett makes sure I'm dressed properly for the occasion.
(Paul Damen)

I never was very good at this hide-and-seek lark!
(Trevor Allen)

Word spreads

A bishop visited a Norfolk village church and found a smaller than usual congregation.

"Did you tell them I was coming?" he asked the old verger.

"No, ole partner," he replied, "but news must he'got out somehow."

Quick wits for an Army reject

When National Service was in force, a young man from rural Norfolk was called up. He pleaded very poor eyesight. Indeed, he failed all the usual tests. Finally, the examiner held up a dustbin lid and said: "Tell me, lad, what's this?"

The lad blinked and replied: "Well, ole bewty, thass either a two-bob bit or half-a-crown."

That did the trick.

He was not accepted – and went off to celebrate with a trip to the cinema in Norwich.

He hadn't been sitting there long when, to his horror, the examiner came in and sat next to him. They recognised each other.

Quick as a flash, the rejected conscript exclaimed: "Am I on the right bus for Corpusty?"

Lemon aid

Henry goes to confession and says: "Bless me, Father, for I have sinned. Last week I went with seven different women."

The priest replied: "Take seven lemons, squeeze them all into a glass and drink the juice."

"Will that cleanse me of sin?"

"No," said the priest, "but it won't half take that smile off your face."

Old bishops never die — you mitre known that!

Mixed emotions

A Norfolk woman wasn't satisfied with the quality of milk supplied by a local farmer. She sent her son with two tins for it.

The farmer asked why. "Please, sir," said the boy, "Mum say will yew put water in one tin an' milk in th'uther. She'll mix it harself."

Dereham town centre as I recall it most fondly. That pub under the town sign is where I supped one of my first pints of brown and mild.

Lot of difference

The Sunday School teacher was describing how Lot's wife looked back and turned into a pillar of salt.

Little Jason interrupted and announced triumphantly: "My mummy looked back once while she was driving — and she turned into a telegraph pole!"

Picturesque scene from Wroxham in the 1920s. Boats and bungalows in harmony.

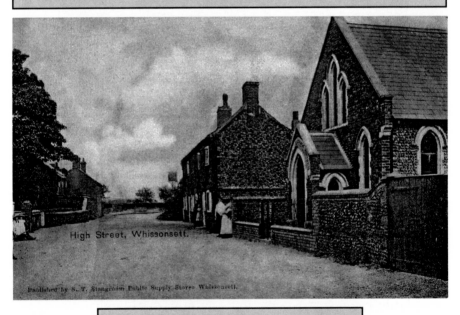

Whissonsett High Street in a more sedate era.

Old archaeologists never die — they just become entrenched.

FOND FAREWELL TO TEACHER 'TOJO'

The recent death of Ike "Tojo" Jones at 94 has prompted a flood of memories and anecdotes among generations of old boys of Hamond's Grammar School at Swaffham.

He taught PE and geography at the school from 1931 to 1958 with a break for war service with the RAF on the Cocos Islands in the Indian Ocean. I survived three years of his stern but fair insistence that there were interesting places beyond Norfolk's boundaries.

He moved on to teach at Wymondham College and Thorpe Grammar School before retiring at 60. He often stressed at our old boys' reunions that he spent more time in retirement than in the classroom.

To mark his 90th birthday in 1996, former pupils presented him with a mounted silver-painted gym shoe as an affectionate reminder of the Sword of Damocles suspended above so many over the years. It brought a cheerful request for the gold-painted partner when he reached his century.

Ted Heath, secretary of the Old Hamondians' Association, said Ike inspired respect and affection. "A certain amount of corporal punishment was allowed in his day but he never abused the power. It was rarely needed, though sometimes threatened, and when it was threatened towards some miscreant the rest of the class would be trying to hide their smiles."

Born in Llanelli and a geography student at Aberystwyth University, he was, inevitably, a rugby man, but deeply regretted some modern changes in the game, like "hoisting" in the line.

My abiding memory of Mr Jones concerns his look of utter bewilderment when I came up with a reasonable description of an ox-bow lake in answer to an unexpected question.

That kept me out of the firing line for nearly a month.

(March, 2000)

Melton Constable railway station when it was known as "the Crewe of Norfolk" and the Midland and Great Northern Joint Railway gloried in the name of the "Muddle and Get Nowhere". Enthusiasts these days say it is "Missed and Greatly Needed".

Sea Palling, one of the places to feel the wrath of the North Sea in the 1953 floods when an abnormally high tide and vicious winter gale brought death and destruction.

My flirtation with the pop world as lead vocalist with Captain Boyton's Benefit Band in the Swinging 1960s at least proved I could be a good judge of a song.

Old friends enjoy a mardle at the Tunstead Trosh, a celebration of old farming ways.

Old corn merchants never die – they just go out on their ears

It hasn't changed much over the years — apart from a massive increase in parked cars. The attractive heart of Castle Acre.

Palgrave pupils and teachers take the air outside their village school near Diss.

Sports Minister Denis Howell gives the EDP's reporter the line-up he'd suggest for the Canaries' next game.

Trouble ahead

Tom was up before the local magistrates. He had struck the road foreman on the head with his shovel after an argument as to how a stretch of road should be repaired to prevent a recurring puddle every time it rained.

The chairman of the bench asked Tom exactly why he had hit the foreman on the head.

"Well, yer honner, we wunt gettin' nowhere, so I thowt thass where the trubble lie!"

Old football managers never die — they just keep on thinking outside the box

One minute he was dozing in Yarmouth . . .

The annual outing from the village pub to Yarmouth was drawing to a close.

Some of the party were finding their way back to the bus when one of them noticed a darts team regular sprawled out on the beach clearly the worse for drink.

"Wuh, there's ole Harry!" he exclaimed. "We'd better lift 'im inter the bus."

He was still tipsy when the bus arrived home, so it was decided to rouse him under the village pump. "Now are yew fit enuff ter walk hoom?" they asked.

"Walk hoom?" Harry bellowed, "I wunt even on this 'ere bloomin' outin'. I wuz on a week's holiday wi' my missus!"

Heavens above

Ezra was odd-job man on a Norfolk farm. He was constantly hustled by all and sundry, particularly by the farmer.

Ezra died and went above. Several years later the farmer took the same route, and after passing through the golden gates he bumped into Ezra.

"How are yew a'gittin' on, ole partner?" he asked.

Ezra fixed him with a serious stare and said: "Dew yew git on wi' yar own tarsks, marster. I'm on the staff up here!"

Good man's smell

A true story from Norfolk in the days before mains water. A lad was sent home from school with a note demanding that he be washed. The indignant mother sent him straight back with this written reply:

"Deer Miss,

Yew hev sent our Billy home because yew say he smell. Well, let me tell you I send him ter school ter be larnt not smelt. Ennyway, he smell jist like his father smell. But there, yew bein' an ole maid, I dunt spooze yew know what a good man smell like!"

Meaning is all too clear

The young lad was caught by his teacher saying a very naughty word.

"Peter," she scolded, "You must not use that word. Where on earth did you hear it?"

"Please Miss, my dad said it," replied the boy.

"Well, that doesn't matter. I don't suppose you even know what it means."

"Oh yis, I dew . . . that mean the car wunt start."

Old carpet-makers never die — they just make a nice pile on the floor.

Sorry, but no repeat performances...

A Norfolk vicar was invited to speak at the Rotary Club's monthly lunch. A reporter from the local newspaper was present at the meal.

After his talk full of light-hearted anecdotes, the vicar begged the reporter not to print too many of his tales as he wished to use them at future local functions.

To the clergyman's utter dismay, when he opened the newspaper a few days later he found the reporter had written: "The vicar made an excellent speech – but most the stories he told cannot be repeated here."

Cabbage count

A Norfolk gardener kept his horticultural cards close to his chest.

A neighbour peered over the fence and asked: "How many cabbages he' yew got planted out there?"

"Half as many as I want."

"Wuh, how the davil many dew yew want, then?"

"Twice as many as woss there now."

A brief confusion

Overheard in a local store packed with festive shoppers:

"Men really hate grey, shabby underwear."

"So why do they wear it?"

Demented arithmetic

A teacher in a Norfolk village school received the following letter from the mother of one of her pupils:

"Deer Miss. Please dunt give Charlie no more hoomwork. That sum abowt how long that'd take a man ter walk 40 times rownd Swaffham Markit cawsed his father ter miss a whool day's work.

"An' then when he'd walked it yew marked the sum rong."

A tricky customer

Horry was always being teased by other village lads.

One of their favourite games was to show how stupid he was by giving him the choice of picking a 20p piece or a 10p piece.

He always chose the 10p piece, sending the bullies into fits of mocking laughter.

"He's thick," they yelled, "he pick the 10p cors thass bigger!"

The local shopkeeper watched this trick being carried out many time before taking Horry to one side.

"I'm sure you must know 10p isn't worth as much as 20p just because it's bigger?" he queried.

"Cors I dew," beamed Horry, "but if I stopped pickin' the 10p, wuh, they'd stop playin' the trick."

Old pigeon fanciers never die – they just go aloft.

Harvesting the old-fashioned way with real horse-power at the heart of it all

Foliage frames the Black Horse at Castle Rising, near King's Lynn.

The Black Horse Hotel, Castle Rising

GETTING TO THE HEART OF NORFOLK SQUIT

Strange to relate, but in all my years at grammar school in Swaffham I never set foot inside the Sacred Heart Convent nearby.

Well, I made full amends for this glaring omission on my Norfolk rounds with a packed day at the school's festival of books and writers, colourfully staged and impeccably organised.

I was invited to give four hour-long talks to different age groups about my career. So there was plenty of scope for featuring the local dialect.

Enthusiastic pupils sorted out words from "botty" to "squit", had a go at reading aloud extracts from the Boy John Letters and formed impromptu choirs for rousing renditions of The Singing Postman's famous anthem, Hev Yew Gotta Loight, Boy?

One girl smiled broadly as she told me "mawkin" was a scarecrow. She should know ... as she lived in Mawkin Cottage. Another girl was equally forthright with the same question directed in another group later on. It was her sister!

I also challenged the youngsters to write the opening lines of a novel set in Norfolk, just enough to entice the reader into wanting to know more. This drew a big and lively response full of surprises and vivid imaginations.

I enjoyed my school dinner and tour of impressive new facilities, including a theatre. Sister Francis, the school's energetic and visionary head, clearly relishes all challenges of modern education ... like finding room for a little bit of squit!

(March, 2004)

Country calm and charm at Starston in south Norfolk. Arnold Wesker, who put the county on an international stage with his play Roots, married a girl from this village.

Hickling Staithe waiting for a Broadland rush.

Playwright Arnold Wesker, who put Norfolk on an international stage with Roots, warms up for a special week of programmes in his honour with me at BBC Radio Norfolk.

Half-time report

An old friend with an impish sense of humour prompted laughter in his local travel agent's shop.

"Which half is Hellesdon going to be in?" he asked. Mystified looks. So he repeated the question. "Sorry, but I don't understand" came the reply.

"Well, you've got a sign in your window advertising trips from the airport — and it says: 'Norwich to Split.' I repeat, which half is Hellesdon going to be in?"

Old crab fishermen never die — they just go to pot.

Brooke Village.

Brooke, seven miles south of Norwich, makes the most of traffic-free days.

Dad knows best

A village schoolmaster taking a class in history asked: "Who signed the Magna Carta?"

Little Bertie replied immediately: "Please sir, I dint."

Next day the schoolmaster met Bertie's dad and said: "Your little lad amused me and the class yesterday when I asked who signed the Magna Carta and he said: "Please sir, I dint"

Dad smiled and replied: "The little beggar, I bet he did!"

Old psychic mediums never die — or at least that's what my great-great-great-great-great-great grandmother told me.

Farmhand's load of Norfolk logic

A classic example of Norfolk logic in this yarn from Norman Suggate, of Sheringham.

A farmer engaged a new hand whose first job was to take a horse and cart into the field to fetch two loads of cattle beet out of the clamp and take them to the barn for winter feeding.

The farmer thought the chap was a long time coming back, but reckoned he had missed him when he brought the first load.

However, the lad turned up and the farmer asked if indeed this was his first load.

"Blarst, no," he replied. "Thass my second load. I'm now a'gorn back arter the fust one."

Surely not an inflated tale?

Charlie was showing a party of tourists round Yarmouth. He pointed out the spot where Lord Nelson supposedly threw a gold sovereign across the River Yare.

"That's impossible," said a tourist, "no one could throw a coin that far."

"Ah, but yew hev ter remember," explained Charlie, "money went a rare lot farther in them days."

It was a stool order when this town boy went a-milkin'

A shortage of jobs in the town meant the boy had to look for work on a farm.

The foreman told him to milk a cow, handing over stool and bucket. An hour later, the boy returned dirty and sweaty. He had the bucket in one hand and a broken stool in the other.

"Gittin' the milk wuz easy," he explained. "Hardest part wuz a'mearkin' th'ole cow sit on the stewl."

Good guess

During his talk to the children, the young curate asked: "What is grey, has a bushy tail and gathers nuts in the autumn?"

Little Ernie at the back raised his hand: "I know th'arnser orter be Jesus — but that dew sound wholly like a squirrel ter me."

Old professors never die — they simply lose their faculties.

Don't be late

From the parish magazine: "At our meeting on Friday, November 14th, the subject will be 'Heaven — how do we get there?'

"Transport available at 7.15 pm from bus stop opposite the King's Head."

Skip notes how time flies while chatting on air with three old newspaper colleagues. Rolling back the years are (left to right) Great Yarmouth photographer Les Gould, former Eastern Evening News editor Bob Walker and Skip's much respected sports editor Ted Bell.

Old crossword compilers never die — they just move to 16 down, 21 across.

Skip and Norwich Theatre Royal legend Dick Condon share a handshake
and laughs galore after another mardle on the wireless.

Boxing clever

A boy on a Norfolk farm had the cheek to ask his master for a
Christmas box.

The farmer put his hand in his pocket and asked: "Let's see,
how much did I give you last year?"

"Noffin'" said the boy.

"Right," said the farmer, "I'll give you the same this year — but
next year don't ask me."

Old butchers never die — they just go on to another joint.

South Green Road, Mattishall.

Mattishall, now so much bigger and busier, makes room for a horse and cart.

Give a hoot

An owl kept Elijah awake at night, making no end of a row while sitting on his plum tree.

"How's that ole owl a'dewin' 'Lijah?"

"Still kickin' up a bloomin' duller all night."

A few mornings later, the same question ..."How's that ole owl a'dewin', 'Lijah?"

"Oh, I're sucked him in ...... "

"Wodyer dew, shoot it?"

"No, I cut the bludder tree down!"

Old insurers never die — it's not part of their policy.

Mr Vout the Bradenham baker on his horse-drawn rounds a few furlongs ago
and Frederick Archer of Wendling delivering meat by horse and cart

Old bakers never die — they knead the dough too much!

THERE'S LOOT IN THEM THERE FOOTPRINTS!

Why does the sight of a film or television crew send our tourism chiefs into such a lather of great expectations?

"Wow!" they cry, "this is the sort of publicity money simply cannot buy!" as a pretty actress leaves her dainty footprints in the sands of Holkham Beach.

"Blimey!" they exclaim, "we can do a big commercial tie-up with the flip-flop people!" as Robinson Crusoe wanders ashore at Winterton.

"Help!" they call, "He does have eyes like red saucers!" as Black Shuck enjoys a midnight rehearsal for a new version of Hound of the Basketmeals.

Golden opportunities on every reel to lure thousands of extras to the very spots where make-believe becomes .... bigger and bolder make-believe.

Where will it all end? Can the Matlaske Falcon nest in peace? Is Citizen Cane heading for Cantley? Will Scroby Dick find true happiness?

As we ponder such important questions at least we know priorities are sorted. One leading light on the Norfolk tourist trail made that abundantly clear as he sized up "Seahenge" off the coast at Holme.

"A structure of this importance cannot be allowed to disappear because it would be a major draw for people from all over the country" he trumpeted.

That sort of positive thinking must ensure money is found to preserve this magic circle. Not because it is one of the most astounding discoveries in the history of Norfolk, but because it has real tourism potential.

Roll on summer and even more footprints in the sand.

(January, 1999)

The Crown Inn at Little Dunham in the 1920s. Landlord Edward Newman sees a couple of satisfied customers on their way. (Litcham Historical Society).

Youngsters at Lexham in mid-Norfolk take a break from classes in the early 1900s.

Plenty of activity outside Great Dunham Post Office and it wasn't even pension day! (Litcham Historical Society)

Gardens and Tower, Yarmouth.

Great Yarmouth's Revolving Tower, built in 1897 at 125 feet tall. Visitors entered a cage which slowly turned while ascending to give a marvellous all-round view. It was demolished during the Second World War and used for scrap.

Double delight

The vicar had been invited to lunch. The two small sons of the household were tearful because in order to feed him in the manner expected, two of the backyard roosters had been killed.

Silently, they sat through the meal while the vicar tucked in. As the family dutifully saw him off, the last of the roosters perched on the garden wall gave a loud "Cockadoodle-doo!"

"My word," exclaimed the vicar, "what a proud bird he is!"

One of the lads, unable to contain himself any longer, blurted out: "An' so he should be, Ravrund ... he're got tew sons in the ministry!"

Old coffee makers never die — they're far too full of beans.

DECEPTIONS

What brought the smell of boarding-houses back
I cannot say. The air was hot and lathery as soap,
when suddenly the room felt full of presences
and there we stood, as shadow as smoke.

And half the day was changed because one sense
picked up the odour of a place where holidays were spent
when I was six. There, on a sultry afternoon,
I saw myself a child again, transfixed.

I watched my father first unpack each case,
then mother test the wash-jug on its stand. I did not know
one week could last so long, or fifty years be lost
as summers are in mislaid photographs.

Somewhere the sea was waiting, while the house
(with musty walls and many-patterned stains) reminded us
its rooms were built for strangers who would not
be staying longer than a week, though smell remains.

I climbed on to a chair to see how near
we were to beaches, waves and rocks. Too far I fear to get
full benefit from days I'd lived for all the year;
I knew at six how disappoints hurt.

I closed my door, know how easily
we let such distances outstrip a need to be elsewhere,
for when I smelt again that sea-world weight of salt,
I was the only one left standing there.

Edward Storey

A memory of Yarmouth, about 1938

Duke Sayer with Peggy (white face) and Beauty on 1942 ploughing duties at Hingham.

Harrowing near Acle ... a typical study from Clifford Temple's collection

General dealer Edward Hutton on his North Walsham and district rounds.

Horse Power

Sugar beet harvesting the old-fashioned way at Easton, near Norwich (Clifford Temple)

Harvest scene at Bawburgh with a spot of glamour (Clifford Temple)

Man, horse and cart almost disappear under a mountain of straw (Clifford Temple).

A horseman riding by … a classic country portrait (Clifford Temple).

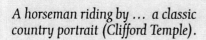

MY NORFOLK HERO

He was not a politician or a soldier or an earl
He didn't own a castle or a hall
His knowledge of the sciences left much to be desired
And of the classics he knew nothing at all.

Not a viscount or a marquis or a writer of good books
Not a singer or an actor of the owner of good looks
He didn't go to Oxford or wear an old school tie
But he left his mark on Norfolk though the world had passed him by.

He appeared a quiet sort of chap under the public gaze
His work was seen and noted and sometimes short of praise
But he hardly ever gave a thought of what he might have been
Not even an archbishop or a canon or a dean.

From dawn till dusk he plied his trade
Well loved by one and all
For he swept the streets of Reepham
And the hinder parts of Salle.

Tom Dack

One day in the park at Clenchwarton
Two lovers sat on a bench, courten,
Their hearts were so full
They dint see the bull
As he tossed them both o'er the fence, snorten!

Feeling better

A rather deaf old lady, who also suffered from poor sight, complained of feeling unwell. Her grandson called the doctor.

After he left, the grandson, raising his voice, said: "Well, Grandma, how are you feeling now?"

"A little better. It was nice o'the wicker ter call."

"But Grandma that was the doctor, not the vicar …"

"Well, blarst me!" exclaimed the old lady, "I wuz a'thinkin' he wuz a bit familiar!"

A Victorian mawther from Caister
Burst from the stays what encased her
But a gallant young knight
Upon seeing her plight
Quickly shoved it all back and relaced 'er!

Old vampires never die — they just grow long in the tooth.

My seat of learning for seven years — the old Hamond's Grammar School at Swaffham. The school has gone — but the impressive building still looks out towards the market place.

Hunstanton Pier, built in 1870, was destroyed in a heavy storm on the night
of January 11, 1978. So it was still there when I went to the resort on Sunday
School outings in the late 1940s and early 1950s.

Blakeney Quay — always a magnet for coastal visitors and local sailors.

On the receiving end for a change... Clifford Temple, photographic recorder of Norfolk's heritage, shows his tractor-driving skills.

A step in the right direction

A Norfolk farmer was waiting for his men to arrive for work on a very frosty morning. One chap had to walk two miles across the fields.

The farmer asked him why he was late. The man replied: "That bloomin' footpath wuz so slippery evra time I took a step forrard I slipped back two."

"Well," said the farmer, "how did you get here then?"

The man replied: "Blarst, I tanned rownd an' went hoom!"

Old nostalgia buffs never die — they just keep living in the past.

Mill Road, Ingham

All quiet on the Ingham front. This village near Stalham, is celebrated for its picturesque cricket ground among the trees,

Caught out

They were a man short at a village cricket match. A keen spectator was enlisted to make up the numbers.

He was sent out to long-on. As the field was on a slope, he was out of sight of the pitch. Apart from throwing the ball in now and again, he didn't have much to do.

After a while a massive hit was sent towering in his direction. He caught the ball and ran up the hill shouting: "I caught it! I caught it!"

The batsman glared angrily at him. "You idiot!" he yelled. "They were all out 15 minutes ago. We are batting now!"

Old numismatists never die — they stay in circulation, to coin a phrase.

Norfolk and Dereham cricketer Barry Battelley teasing the opposition. One of a talented sporting set of brothers, his all-round skills and jovial character shone out over many seasons.

Robin Huggins lit up the Norfolk county and club cricket scene with his graceful style and timing.

VILLAGE VOICE

Written and presented by Keith Skipper
Mid Norfolk Sunday Cricket League Centenary Dinner
at Lakenham, Sunday, September 13th, 1998.

I carn't believe them years hev parst
A hundred onnem? wuh! no, cor blarst,
That only seem a few summers back
Since we put Elmham on the rack.
They wuz hot stuff in them there days,
Afore both wars they earned their praise.
But, bor, they found us full o' fire
And we won easy. I ent no liar.
Boy Harbert, him what fed the hoss,
Say: "Put 'em in if yew win the toss."
He hed a feelin' the ball would fly.
That did — like a bludder cokernut shy!
Lumpy Laycock and Blimpo Bevan
They hossed 'em out for twetty-seven.
Time we batted the pitch hed died
An' our opening pair hed an easy ride.
Boy Harbert sit there wi' a gret ole grin:
"Theeryare, I told yer ter put 'em in".
Mind yew, that boy wunt allus right.
I remember Beetley on Wennsday night.
We put 'em in, like Harbert say,
An oh my lor! they med us pay!
They clouted two hundred and sixty-eight,
We med fifty — and got hoom late.
Boy Harbert din't want a ding o' the lug
So he went to New Inn ter fill the jug.
We larnt the young hellyun ter say "Put 'em in",
Cors we drank all the beer and sent him agin.
Now Chunky, our spinner, was good at teasin'em
He once took eight for sixteen at Weasenham.
But he liked a pint afore he'd start,
He reckun that give him hope and heart.

Now we went to Mileham when they wuz the best
In the early twenties, the rest wunt no test.
We git there early — and what dew yew think?
Pub was shut, and we coont git a drink.
Chunky he bowl three overs, thass all,
Wi' fifteen wides and twelve no-ball.
"I'm dehydrearted!" he shout. Thass clear
Chunky's no good wi'out his beer.
Pletty of others I kin call ter mind
As memories flow o' the cricketing kind.
Ryburgh, Rougham, Shipdham, Salle,
We hed our moments aginst 'em all.
Foulsham, Lexham, West Acre tew,
Some onnem ole clubs and some onnem new.
Summers hev gone, with a lot o' the lads
Who sat near the hedge a'bucklin' their pads
They come orf the farms, fearces all brown,
An' played the game till the sun went down.
They swore, they laughed an' went hoom tight
Arter drownin' sorrers late inter the night,
New we kin put orl them innin's tergether,
All kinds o'lads, all kinds o'weather.
All sorts o'pitches, an' umpires no doubt,
But still they're got to a hundred not out.
I carnt believe them years hev parst.
A hundred onnem? wuh! no! cor blarst,
That only seem a few overs back
Since we put Longham on the rack!

Mileham & Lexham ,early 1900s.

Stanfield & Mileham, about 1920.

An amorous vicar from Docking
Met a mawther whose morals were shocking
An encounter which led
As the EDP said
To a case of double unfrocking

NOSTALGIA

When hedges were hedges, and men were men,
And dairymaids blushed o'er the lea,
When horses pulled through meadow and fen,
And the molecatcher was late for his tea.

When the tied cottage window winked its hello.
And the lilac sang on the breeze,
When Old Mother Sankey went to hearth with a bellow,
And scrubbed brick floors on her knees.

When ragged-trousered urchins wrote on their slates,
And pulled chunks of ice from their hair,
When turnip soup spilled over the plates,
And the workers made all their own beer.

While all of this was carving its way
Through the bark of hope and time,
I was out hunting in red coat so gay,
And thinking "Isn't rural life sublime?"

Joshua Mace,
Circa 1954

Old rowers never die — they just keep on sticking their oar in

All set for a night on the town.

Old after-dinner speakers never die — they just go on and on and on and on …

Vital fixture

A motorist pulled up in deepest Norfolk and asked the old road-mender: "Where does this road go to, my good man?"

The old boy scratched and ruminated before responding: "That dunt go nowhere — that stay here where thass wanted."

A charming scene starring Paston Mill — still attracting wide attention on the outskirts of Mundesley.

Good example

An old man and a younger one were muckspreading on a field when a farmer, who had been watching them from the gate, walked over for a chat.

"He said to the young man: "I're bin a'watchin' yew an' I hev noticed the ole man is spreadin' tew forkfuls ter yar one."

"Yis, marster," said young George. "I keep tellin' the silly ole fewl but he tearke no notice o'me."

Old doctors never die — they just get out of practice.

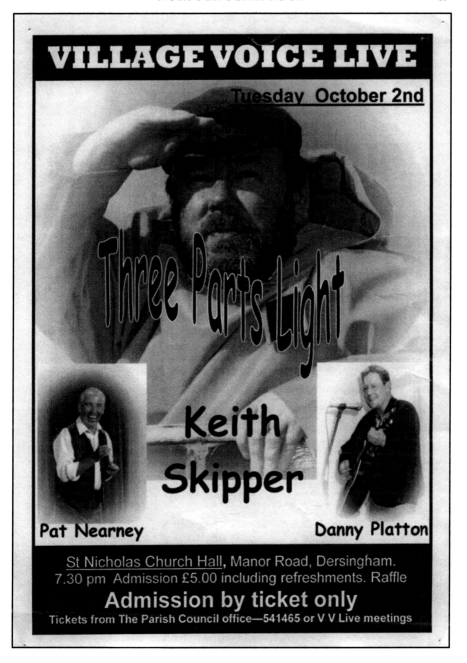

Old yachtsmen never die — they just keel over.

TORKIN' PROPER

It's time to do away with this myth that we have an all-purpose regional accent.

An academic specialising in speech recognition systems was in Lowestoft recently collecting samples of "East Anglian dialect" in a bid to help computers understand people. I would have thought some scope remained to sort things out the other way round … but that may just be me.

Professor Martin Russell, of Birmingham University, presumably knows the distinction between dialect and accent; one is what we say, the other is how we say it.

I have stressed many times that while Norfolk and Suffolk carry many similarities in dialect and delivery, they are different enough to warrant individual treatment and respect.

Indeed, "torkin' Norfolk" and "torkin' Norwich" immediately betray the fact that county and city sounds can vary considerably. There are many shades across a place the size of Norfolk.

It's wrong to suggest someone has an East Anglian tone just as it's folly to lump together all West Country or all Northern voices.

Another question worth posing … what exactly do we mean by East Anglia? Is it Norfolk, Suffolk and a bit of Essex? Or should it also take in Lincolnshire, Cambridgeshire and Huntingdonshire?

I firmly contend it is up to individual counties to complain, cajole, campaign, canvass and convince media moguls and others who constantly go astray that they really must do better.

(March, 2003)

*One of the highlights of my newspaper career —finding a new friend at a
Great Yarmouth fete in the mid-1960s. I called him Gladly
(my cross-eyed bear).*

Old plumbers never die — they just go clean round the bend.

GRESSENHALL

(On a family visit to Norfolk Rural Life Museum)

I heard the call from Gressenhall
Of paupers on the parish
Their dining hall in workhouse tall
Has seen an era perish
Sad inmates gone their crying done
And stigma peeled from door
Old farming's sun is setting on
A world we now hold dear
They've come inside but not to hide
Those weather-beaten faces
A tumbril ride still carries pride
And horse power tethers forces
Weed and hoe then scare the crow
Bring all the harvests home
They heed the call from Gressenhall
To sing a rural hymn:
"We plowed them filds an' scattered
Some good muck on th' land
But now we're sort o' shattered
Yew walk — we'll garp an' stand!"

Keith Skipper
August, 1992

Derek James

Contact Derek James at derek.james@archant.co.uk
or call (01603) 772420

Keith Skipper publishes his 25th book and it's full of Norfolk ge

We really are a suspicious lot, bo

IT WAS in the 1920s that travelling author H V Morton wrote: "Norfolk is the most suspicious county in England.

"In Devon and Somerset, men hit you on the back cordially; in Norfolk they look as though they would like to hit you over the head — 'till they size you up," he wrote in his 1927 book, In Search of England.

He explained that for centuries, the North Folk of East Anglia were accustomed to meeting stray Vikings on lonely roads who had just waded ashore from the long boats.

"Good morning, bor!" said the Vikings. "Which is the way to the church?"

"What d'ye want to know for?" was the Norfolk retort.

"Well, we thought about setting fire to it!"

H V Morton added: "You will gather that Norfolk's suspicion of strangers, which is an ancient complex bitten into the East Anglian through centuries of bitter experience, is well grounded and should never annoy the traveller."

This story is just one of the gems included in a new book called Normal for Norfolk, the latest offering from our top dumpling, Keith Skipper.

More than 75 years on, Keith writes: "Rape and pillage and setting fire to churches may not be top of the current invasion wish-list, but ugly developments, through-the-roof house prices and gradual destruction of the spirit of a people and a place are surely wicked affronts to Norfolk's precious 'dew diffrunt' doctrine.

"Modern Vikings, wading ashore with their Range Rovers, Agas, Barbours, Puffas, stuffed olives, black truffles and green wellies can be just as dangerous as their horns-and-helmets predecessors," said Keith.

BOOK SIGNING

■ Keith will be signing copies of his new book in Jarrold's, Norwich, on Saturday, December 6 from noon to 2pm.

What he has done in this book is put together a whole string of stories and yarns about Norfolk and its people — warts an' all.

"After more than 40 years of writing and talking about my native county for a living, this is the proper time to take stock, to hand out a few home truths and to prove I have been paying attention most of the way," says Keith.

And he does just that.

This is his 25th book and one of his most thoughtful and controversial. It reflects his deep and genuine passion for Norfolk.

■ Normal for Norfolk is published by Halsgrove and costs £12.95.

NOR
FOR
NOR
Keith
Skipp
25th b

THE COPYCAT TRAIL

I had to smile the other day — and not just because it adds to your face value.

Yet another of those pesky surveys making outrageously broad claims on wafer-thin evidence told us that working while travelling by train is now regarded as normal.

Apparently, no less than 350 business commuters confided in researchers with one-track minds. I think I saw 349 of them decked out with laptops and mobile phones on my last train trip to London.

Funny, but I don't recall a single inquiry during the seven years I and many others used the old Dereham — Swaffham stretch to build up a head of steam in the name of delayed homework. We may not have invented such compartmental thinking in that golden age (1955-62) before Bully Beeching tore up our lines. But it surely came to a local peak on Monday mornings ...

Any researcher would have been flattened in the rush to find the clever-dick with a full set of algebra or geometry answers nestling in the bottom of his satchel. A whole Woodbine and half a Wagon Wheel were prime bartering fodder.

Every subject had its travelling kingpin — and price — but there were occasional calamities when nine identically wrong theorem exercises queued up for inspection on teacher's desk. I got caught down the copycat trail so often it eventually became more fun and less hassle to make up my own mistakes.

A morning diversion brought a whiff of potential romance to our cheat-day returns. Grammar Grubs heading for Swaffham and High School Hussies heading for Dereham gazed longingly at each other as their respective trains passed at Dunham.

Remember, this was long before mobile phones and the joys of texting. So hastily-scribbled notes through hastily-opened windows carried offers of undying affection at least until the weekend.

Suddenly my workrate reached dizzying heights while my pulse stayed normal. I became technical advisor to smitten smoothies whose brains had hit the buffers.

More than a Woodbine beckoned for the maths dunce who could spell "fancy", "heartbeat", and "bikeshed" ... with a "palpitation" thrown in for luck.

(January, 2000)

Size matters

Jacob and Eliza were relaxing in front of the fire as Christmas cards trembled on the mantelpiece above.

Suddenly, the old gal turned to her husband of 65 years and said: "Bor, if I should go afore yew, will yew promise me if yew tearke on sumwun else yew wunt let her wear my clothes?"

"Dunt yew fret, my bewty, cors I wunt" replied Jacob.

"Ennyway, they wunt fit."

Village store with delivery wagon outside at Swanton Morley. The shopkeeper waits for orders.

Right track

Several years ago a city gent was waiting at a little railway halt in Norfolk.

As a porter approached pushing a luggage truck, he hailed him: "I say, my good man, is the next train for Liverpool Street?"

The old porter looked thoughtful for a moment and then quietly replied: "Well, tew are cummin', but yars is the one what stop."

Ideal transport for the Norfolk squit trail (Trevor Allen).

Old midwives never die — they just go from here to maternity.

Long service in our local pulpits

One of the most impressive records in the county was set by the Rev. Bartholomew Edwards when he served as Rector of Ashill for 76 years. He died just nine days short of his 100th birthday.

He never retired, never went away for a holiday and hardly missed a service. Father of the Ashill flock from 1813 until his death in 1889, he buried village folk he had baptised as children.

Nearest I can find to the Edwards record is 72 years of service by the Rev. Louis Norgate at Bylaugh in mid-Norfolk (1836-1908).

James Cory served the parish of Kettlestone, near Fakenham, for 68 years. His father was rector there before him. Philip Candler completed the same number of years at Lamas, near Aylsham, before he died in 1832.

Henry Wilson (Kirby Cane) and Henry Astley (Little Snoring) both did 64 years. Henry Dawson served Bunwell for 63 years while John Coldham (Stockton) and John Fayerman (Geldeston) both clocked up 62.

There are also several examples of outstanding family records. The Boycotts were rectors at Burgh St Peter from 1764 until 1899. Members of the Manning family were continuously rectors of Diss for 138 years, from time of the American War of Independence to the First World War (1778 – 1916).

Canon Walter Herbert Marcon, who moved the original church half a mile to its present position, was Rector of Edgefield for nearly 63 years (1875 – 1937), His father was rector there for 27 years before him, and a great uncle for 19 years before that.

Prior to the Marcons taking over, Bransby Francis ministered in the tumbledown church for 65 years.

Three generations of Cresseners were rectors at West Harling for a span of 134 years from 1596, Henry serving the last 60 of them.

Skip holding forth in a Norfolk pulpit. (Chris Gill)

Cheerful plot

An old Norfolk man was walking through the churchyard in his home village. A friend with him said how well the churchyard looked.

"Yis, that dew" said the old boy, "an' thass where I hope ter be buried one day if I'm alive an' well."

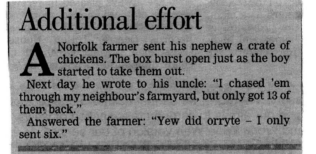

Additional effort

A Norfolk farmer sent his nephew a crate of chickens. The box burst open just as the boy started to take them out.

Next day he wrote to his uncle: "I chased 'em through my neighbour's farmyard, but only got 13 of them back."

Answered the farmer: "Yew did orryte – I only sent six."

Get your own

A rather fastidious man was sitting in a Norwich bus opposite a woman and small boy. The lad kept on sniffing.

At last the chap could stand it no longer. "Does that boy have a handkerchief?" he asked.

"Yis, that he hev," came the reply, "But he ent a'lendin' onnit ter yew!"

Old prime ministers never die — they just hide in the cabinet.

Roving reporter ready for action. Those words in the window sum up Skip's media career perfectly ... creative, flexible and local.

Bright spark

A Norfolk lad went on his first date. His father noticed he was carrying a lantern.

"What are yew a'dewin' wi' that, boy? I dint tearke no lantern when I went a'cortin ...."

"No," replied the boy, "an' just look at what yew come hoom with!"

Old teachers never die — they move to a higher class.

Drilling barley at Hockering with horses again to the fore (Clifford Temple)

Ahead of his time

A commuter moved to the Norfolk countryside. Desperate to catch a train, he called to a farmer busy tending his cows along the lane :"Hey, grandpa, is it okay with you if I take a short-cut across your field? I really must catch the 8.15."

The farmer smiled and replied: "Dew yew go ahid, young marster ... but if my bull see yew, reckun yew might catch the 7.45."

Old housewives never die — they just can't find the time.

Canine counting

A Norfolk farmer wondered how many sheep he had in a particular field. He asked his intelligent sheepdog to count them.

The dog duly carried out the order. "Well, how many?" asked the farmer.

"Forty" replied the dog.

"How can there be 40 when I only bought 38 at market?"

"I know" said the dog, "but I rounded them up for you."

Steady progress on the harrowing front (Clifford Temple).

Old furniture-makers never die — they just pine away.

Plenty of time for a stroll and mardle on a street full of fresh air in Catfield.

A quiet day on New Buckenham's King Street but at least one smart dress on parade.

Old pharmacists never die — they just get dispensed with.

Sloppy language?
Tell me abaht it!

Many of the things that niggle me most are tied up with sloppy verbal communications — and I will not accept that big allowances must be made as our language "continues to evolve in an exciting manner."

For example, I am tired of Norfolk people pretending to come from London when they utter soap-opera banalities Like "Tell me abaht it!" and "That is well out of order, my son!"

Clearly no better than newcomers or holidaymakers from the capital and elsewhere pretending to be hearty natives as they produce an exaggerated "Cor, blarst me, there's a bishy-barny-bee!" on entering the village pub.

The next person to trot out a cloyingly condescending "Bless!" after a straightforward bulletin about Billy's bronchitis or Olive's operation deserves to be smothered in treacle.

Perhaps I can find a spare gallon or two of salt water in which to submerge those who insist on being "really gutted" by some minor setback rather than a dextrous Scottish fishergirl.

I am cheesed off with teashop cacklers who squawk "Sweet enough!" when turning down offers of sugar. I am fed up with signs outside establishments bearing the legend "Dogs welcome with well-behaved owners." Dogs can't read.

Tragic delusions of novelty and humour plague our society, especially in pubs and clubs where "Hey, you guys!" appears to be the sole way of addressing everyone present. I've even heard schoolteachers apply this "cool" epithet to mixed classes.

I despair of folk who use their vehicles as travelling discos, their mobile phones as public announcement systems and their rubbish as street decoration.

Ah, I feel better for that. Now I'll check on my own shortcomings. The wife is consulting her list for a start.

Light fantastic

The teacher was explaining to her Norfolk class the speed of light. "So, even though the sun is about 93 million miles away, its light reaches us in just over eight minutes. Isn't that amazing?" she concluded.

"Nut really," said Horry. "Thass downhill all the bloomin' way!"

Chatting with ice skating stars Jayne Torvill and Christopher Dean at the Royal Norfolk Show.

Funeral thoughts

Two old Norfolk boys watched a hearse roll slowly by.

As it disappeared into the distance, one asked: "Who died, then?"

"Him in the box, I reckon" said the other.

"Yis" mused the first, "driver looked orryte.

Above, a formidable harvesting line-up at Briston with youngsters playing important roles. The lower harvesting squad may have been bolstered by a late call ... as it was considered most unlucky to have 13 faces on parade.

High Street, Walsingham.

Walsingham High Street, so often the scene these days of flocks of pilgrims.

WALSINGHAM

I get a funny feeling in Walsingham
When sun shines on tearooms and guilt
At the end of the pilgrim season
And a torrent more prayer has been spilt
Hedges drip blood-red round Walsingham
The odd tree wears a Calvary frown
It's the heart of the sugar beet season
When green is washed down in brown
The colours of life are all changeless
Though they worship each other in turn
I buy a new postcard of Walsingham
And wait for the year to adjourn
They'll be back to lift crosses in Walsingham
I'll return while the calmness is king
And they're still lifting beet down the sideroads
Where the shrine is mud, sweat and string.

Keith Skipper
October, 1994

Delayed non-reaction

Two Norfolk pensioners were recalling their second world war experiences.

"Horry, dew yew remember them pills they used ter give us in the Air Force ter keep our mynds orff the mawthers?"

"Cum ter think onnit, I dew."

"Well, I reckon myne are beginnin' ter work!"

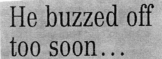

Norfolk logic has just twigged...

A London businessman on holiday in rural Norfolk was chatting to a village resident. The conversation came round to bird life and habits.

Pointing to a rook's nest high in the trees beyond the church, the local said: "Dew yew know, sar, them there rooks only use tew sorts o' twigs ter build thar nests?"

"Most interesting," replied the visitor. "Would you know what sort they are?"

"Yis," answered the local. "Straight 'uns an' bent 'uns!"

He buzzed off too soon...

A henpecked husband finally did something without his wife's permission.

He dropped dead. She was devastated. No one to moan at, to harass and torment. Her neighbour was sympathetic.

"I can tell you're missing poor Jack," she said.

The widow wiped away a tear and replied: "Oh yes, it seems only yesterday he came up the path, opened the front door and stood there . . . letting two flies in."

Hector just has nowhere to run

The Norfolk farmer was complaining to Hector, one of his workers, about his habitual tardiness.

"Strange," he said, "you're always late and you live just across the road.

"Charlie lives three miles away, and yet he's always on time."

"Noffin' strange 'bowt that atorl," replied Hector.

"If Charlie's late in the mornin', he kin hurry. If I'm late, I'm here."

Old railwaymen never die — they just stay on track.

NORFOLK MOMENTS

Felt when the reeds blown backwards
curl their tresses of broadland hair,
combed out, parted, swept up to fringe
the freckled face of the dimpled stream.

Seen when the marsh swan settles
scudding her great span onto the water.
Her whiteness breaking the surface into ripples
lapping the lilies in supple circles.

Heard when the cries of the curlews
sailing millwards, soar home in the evening,
throating their curved-bill calls over moorland
over the holls and deeks of the fenland.

Smelt when the rip of the plough blade
coils and curves a lip upon the furrow.
When the tang from the moist torn turf
is turned from the glistening earth.

Tongued when the rush of threshed grain
filters down the gullet of the sack.
When the milled corn powdered and baked
is browned to the cult of the taste.

Dennis Marshall

Skip pays tribute to a world boxing champion from his home village as he takes "seconds out" at Jem Mace's memorial in Beeston churchyard.

Mildred Symonds, 86, leads the way on a proud day for my home patch of Beeston. She hands a scroll to Tony Whales, vice-chairman of the parish council, transferring ownership of the village sign from the jubilee committee to the village in 1977. (Eastern Daily Press).

WEYBOURNE VILLAGE.

Weybourne, where former Prime Minister John Major has a Norfolk home, in much quieter times.

SIDESTRAND.—CHURCH FARM

Horse and wagon take centre-stage at Church Farm in Sidestrand, the small village near Cromer.

Mrs Blunt

A Norfolk man wanted to be "buried decent" and to this end he had his coffin made some years before it was likely to be needed. He kept it in the front room.

During a serious illness this clergyman paid a visit. The patient told him all was ready ... "Dew yew go an'see that there corffin." The vicar did so and told the man's wife it was indeed a very handsome coffin.

"Yis, I spooz thass orryte," said the old lady. "But I'll be glad ter see the back onnit. That dew clutter the plearce up so."

Double-act was in a spin

A top showbusiness agent passed a building site and saw a man do five back somersaults and a head spin.

The agent called out: "Brilliant! I'll book you for the summer season at Yarmouth!" The man replied: "You'll have to book Paddy as well. He's the one who burned my backside with his blowtorch."

First impressions

A first excursion from Norfolk to London can be quite an invigorating experience.

One old boy of 82 had never been outside Fakenham. On arrival at Liverpool Street, he was too afraid to venture any further.

However, after several hours on the station he developed a thirst and went a few yards up the road to find a pub. The barmaid served him with a pint of mild.

He looked her straight in the eye and exclaimed: "I expect yew'll be funny busy terday, miss. There's savrul onus come up from Fearkenham ...... "

*Skip and sports desk colleague Colin Bevan meet Princess
Alexandra as she opens Prospect House in 1970 — a
brand new base for our local press.*

*Final Edition — Skip with farewell gifts and colleagues as
he leaves the full-time newspaper world in the late 1970s.
Evening News editor Bob Walker makes the presentation
while looking on are (left to right) Pete March, Bryan
Stevens, Clive Harris, Keith Peel, Richard Futter, Peter
Franzen and Peter Bright.*

BIRD OF SPRAY
HOLDS UP PLAY

I've heard some neat excuse for players and officials being late for cricket matches.

"The in-laws were round and I had to help with the washing-up" was one such tale of woe. "Oh, we dropped in at the pub to pay our pontoon and Charlie, who owed us a pint, came in … "and the rest is Saturday lunchtime history.

However, a Sunday fixture in the early 1980s, when I played quite regularly for Caister CC, produced a memorable incident in which a couple of colleagues could point to neither extra time at the sink, nor sinking an extra pint, for rolling up a bit behind time for our Norfolk Junior Cup tie at Old Buckenham.

Mick Jones and umpire Ken Jary had to nip back home and change. They were dive-bombed as they loaded up the car. A passing bird with a wry sense of humour dropped even more than I could manage in a season.

Naturally, the rest of us thought it a really spiffing jape and wondered if this bird of spray was simply depositing an omen.

We were all out for 94. We had a nice tea. Then it rained very heavily and that was that. "See you in a fortnight" they said after we'd shared yarns and refreshment at the White Horse. Then it had to be time to go home to research the strangest example of a bird interfering with a cricket match.

Look no further than April 21st, 1928, when a team at Montagu in South Africa had to suspend play when one of the ostriches near the pitch darted forward and swallowed the ball.

As it was the only one available, the game developed into an ostrich hunt. The bird was captured and its neck massaged and pummelled until it spat out the ball.

Band of Hope — it's rehearsal time for five creative local press reporters making up Captain Boyton's Benefit Band in the swinging 1960s. Left to right — Charlie Catchpole (guitar), David Wakefield (keyboard), Keith Skipper (lead singer), Sid Langley (guitar) and Dick Watts (drums). Fame proved elusive — and the malady lingers on.

Different flock

The Norfolk vicar was preaching a powerful sermon about death and judgement .... "Just think, all you living in this parish will die one day."

Old Charlie in the front pew began to chuckle. After the service the vicar demanded rather sternly: "Now, my good man, why do you find such a serious subject so amusing?"

"Well, my ole bewty," replied Charlie, "I'm just wholly pleased I dunt live in this parish."

Old decorators never die — they're just overcome with emulsion.

LOVED TO DEATH?

How many more reports will it take to convince us that the north Norfolk coast is being loved to death?

We've just been told £122 million is spent each year by visitors along the Snettisham to Weybourne stretch alone, supporting 3,000 jobs. A lot of money, valuable employment — and environmental nightmares as 92 per cent of tourists use cars.

This latest report highlighting such figures says trippers must not be allowed to ruin the beauties they come to see. The report comes from the RSPB.

That must stand for Regular Surrender of Proper Balance. Or even Right, Stop Passing the Buck.

(April, 2000)

A careless old fella from Litcham
Tore his trousers and asked me to stitch'em
I sewed up the flies
Bringing tears to his eyes
And he hurriedly had to unhitchem.

Old disco dancers never die — they just go-go on for ever.

Knocked off top shelf by radical Thomas Paine!

Well, there's always the Booker Prize!

That was my immediate reaction at being pushed off the literary top shelf by radical heavyweight Thomas Paine.

His classic political thriller *Right of Man*, written well over 200 years ago, was chosen by Eastern Daily Press readers as the first volume to find a home in Norwich's Millennium Library in 2001.

My light-hearted tome, *A Load of Old Squit*, first delivered in 1985, came second in this prestigious race after setting the early pace. A shortlist was drawn up from readers' suggestions. It was flattering to be nominated let alone figure in the final reckoning.

I worked overtime to find a connection with Paine, who, as far as can be told, had no truck with honeycarts, dialect or rustic humour. Then it dawned on me … we both cut our writing teeth on Thetford's stirring exploits.

The stay-maker's son was born there in 1737 when the town was a classic "rotten borough." Corruption rife in local politics may well have influenced his own ideas later on. He received a good education at the

Free Grammar School in Bridge Street until he was 13.

I arrived in Thetford fresh from school in 1962 when it was on course to becoming the fastest-growing town in Britain. As a cub reporter on the Thetford and Watton Times, I soon learned that "overspill" had

Thetford reflections from the early 1900s.

nothing to do with generous pub landlords while "GLC" owed little to Gressenhall Lacemakers' Club.

My cultural instincts were fed by the local drama society and sports journalism aspirations lifted by coverage of Thetford Reserves' football fixtures at windswept Mundford Road.

I steered clear of writing pamphlets advocating political and social change and I kept views on religion and the monarch to myself. I was too busy making calls at the police station, interviewing golden wedding couples and trying to operate the office teleprinter with one finger.

Suffice to say those days provided a grand grounding for all subsequent years of toil in the Norfolk media vineyard. Thomas Paine went to London when he was 20 — overspill in reverse — and seldom returned. For many years he was disowned by his native town.

Indeed, he had to wait until 18 months or so after my departure to be honoured by a gilded statue outside King's House, paid for by the Thomas Paine Foundation of America in 1964.

Perhaps my only other obvious link with this remarkable writer and thinker concerns his membership of a certain organisation when he settled in Sussex in the 1760s.

My wife says I would have made a perfect colleague for him in the Headstrong Club.

Old lace-makers never die — they just keep bobbin along.

Parish pump politics in North Walsham market place with
"Bruff" Hewitt and Dan Mount.

**Old organists never die — they just keep on pulling out
all the stops.**

ICY RESPONSE

Understatement is at the heart of much Norfolk humour. I happened across this perfect example while leafing through a pile of old magazines.

An old man lived with his son and daughter-in-law in a remote Norfolk village. It was his habit to take an evening glass of ale in the local pub.

His return home was so punctual that the clocks could be set by it. But one bitter night he failed to appear at the fixed time. After nearly an hour his son became apprehensive and went out to look for him.

The poor old chap had walked into a pond and the sides were too slippery for him to clamber out. He'd been floundering about in the icy water for almost an hour. The following conversation took place:

"Arnt yew suffin' cowld, father?"

"I dunt sweat much."

In a spin over fan's function

Several years ago, two Norfolk women were enjoying a cup of tea in the beach café at Mundesley. There was a large fan revolving from the ceiling. The conversation went like this:

First woman (looking up): "Dunt see how that dew that."

Second woman: "How what dew what?"

First woman: "How that curl yer hair."

Second woman: "I dint say that curl yer hair. I say that cule th'air."

Old publishers never die – they just turn down the volume.

CHILLING CHAPTER

A Norfolk tragedy born out of chilling indifference to the bleak mid-winter demanded inspection as I thumbed through some old papers.

Thomas Jones of Themelthorpe, near Foulsham, was out at work when only 12 years old. Compulsory education did not arrive for at least another century.

On January 12th, 1776, he was sent by Richard Palmer to drive some cattle towards London. The weather turned so severe he was told to call off the trip and put up at The Bull in Watton. More snow fell and drifting got worse.

If the cattle did reach the capital it was with another drover. Thomas Jones, with no proper winter clothing, froze to death on Thompson Common.

His master's brother, who was with him, must have been guilty of criminal negligence or at least callous indifference. The boy was not discovered until February 6th. Then it took another 10 days to find someone to bury him. Parish records give no reasons for the delay.

A heart-rending little tale to put all our moans and problems in perspective when the cold winds blow.

HIGH ST. FOULSHAM.(LOOKING SOUTH.)

A group of youngsters in Foulsham look for adventures ... 1920s style.

One of my favourite haunts where time is encouraged to stand still. Heydon — the only village in Norfolk you can enter but not pass through.

End of the school day in Baconsthorpe — and no cars waiting to take the little dears home!

Old bookmakers never die — yes, you can bet on it!

One of my all-time favourites from Norfolk past. Tending the thatch at Attleborough Lodge at Kimberley in 1950. Cecil Dawson is on the right with his friend Kenny Nixon up aloft. The little girl pushing the pram is two-year-old Maureen Dawson. She's now Maureen Davis of Stoke Holy Cross. "When we lived in this incredibly beautiful house, there were no main drains or electricity. We had a water pump and toilet in the garden and oil lamps in the house" she recalls. "We left Attleborough Lodge when I was seven as my father managed to buy a house and find a new job in a nearby village."

Cooling off in Nelson's Brook at Burnham Thorpe, the village where Norfolk's great naval hero was born. His dad was the local rector.

Aldborough Green, near Cromer, remains a popular cricket venue. Perhaps these ducks wanted to send out a message to visiting sides!

RIGHT NAME FOR THE JOB

Any search in Norfolk to find the right name for the job must lead to Jim Smellie, the public health officer who gained national notoriety.

Happily blessed with a keen sense of humour, he chuckled at mentions in the national press and Punch magazine before an appearance on Esther Rantzen's That's Life television show.

A native of Lancashire, he moved to Norfolk in 1949 as deputy chief public health officer and was promoted to the top job in 1960. He died in 1992.

Surely the most gloriously suitable name for a leader of the flock must be the Rev. Ralph Fuloflove. He was rector at West Harling in 1470 and his brass portrait is the oldest memorial in the parish church.

Many will remember when the town of Wells had a butcher named Arthur Ramm, a jeweller and watchmaker called George Goldsmith and a lifeboat coxswain named David Cox.

There was a doctor in Fakenham with the initials JAB — John Ambrose Braithwaite — while Arthur Watts was in charge of the local Eastern Electricity showroom. Mrs Bunn worked in Wagg the Baker's shop while the Finns, John, Spencer and Kevin, were involved in the fish business.

Alec Bull of East Tuddenham worked inevitably as a dairy herdsman around Norfolk and Suffolk. Swaffham fishmonger John Bone was at one time in partnership with George Mackrell of Mattishall.

When a repertory company used to perform at the then Cromer Town Hall Theatre, it was often noted in the programme that certain stage objects were supplied by local firms or people. On one occasion it read "Eggs supplied by A.Bird", a local farmer.

Sir was just as nervous!

I enjoyed my role as court jester at Dereham Learning Festival.

An excuse to roll back the years and roll out favourite yarns always comes as a happy diversion. To have it masquerading as something to do with education is an unlikely bonus.

The town football club's palatial headquarters at Aldiss Park provided a telling clue to big changes since I covered the team's fortunes for the local paper in the early 1960s.

My best line from those days of reporting from The Rec concerned Magpies in green and white ... "most unsuitable nom-de-plumage."

Getting away with that helped persuade me to feather my journalistic nest a few years later by keeping an eye on the Canaries. The rest, as they say, ought to be history.

Talking of lessons, it was a delight to chat with Cyril Nicholls after my stint out in the middle on this return to Dereham. Cyril was games master when I started life at Hamond's Grammar School at Swaffham in September, 1955. He also taught history and geography, enlivening many sessions with colourful sporting anecdotes.

"I started the same day as you" he revealed. An old boy of the school, Cyril launched his teaching career as the new lads of '55 blinked and blustered into a strange new world.

"And I was just as nervous!" added the man who nearly believed me when I claimed to have pace, poise, positional sense and passion on the soccer pitch.

(September, 2001)

Old foresters never die — they just grow alder.

Talent scout — the only excuse for dressing up like this for a stint on stage at Norwich Theatre Royal.

Right idea

The farmer put a notice up outside an orchard packed with fruit. It read: "Please don't pick the fruit as they are for the Harvest Festival."

A few days later he was strolling past the orchard. The trees were empty. All the fruit had been stolen and the notice replaced with: "All is safely gathered in."

Old lingerie salesmen never die — they just slip away

The Cromer and Sheringham Arts Festival 23-31 October

COAST

Keith Skipper
Desert Island Dusks

The Boy Keith waxes lyrical at the Red Lion
with a selection of bedtime reading for a
Norfolk castaway, featuring his favourite books
spanning the years.

Friday 22 October at 7.30pm One night only!
The Red Lion, Cromer £5 - tickets at the door

Old telephonists never die — they just go ex-directory.

Err, can you just run that by me again . . .

An elderly widow and widower on the Norfolk coast had been dating for five years.

Charlie finally asked Mary to marry him and she said yes.

But next morning Charlie couldn't remember what her answer had been. In desperation, he decided to phone her.

"This is very embarrassing," he began, "but when I asked you to marry me yesterday . . . well, this morning I just can't remember what your answer was."

"Oh, I'm ever so glad you called," replied Mary.

"I remember saying yes to someone, but I couldn't remember who it was."

Now you see it, now you don't

Horry took a photograph of his mate Herbert to the chemist.

"I'd like yew ter enlarge this for me," he said, "an' would that be possible ter remove his hat?"

"Certainly, sir, but tell me, which side does the gentleman part his hair?"

"Dunt be ser sorft," exclaimed Horry. "Yew'll see that when yew tearke his hat orff."

This show called for a spin doctor!

A local amateur dramatics group got a bit ambitious and staged their version of King Lear. A review in the local paper indicated how it went:

"Lower Dodman Players performed Shakespeare's King Lear to a full house in the village hall. The only real benefit to be derived from this production is that it can at least clear up the question as to whether the play was written by Shakespeare or Bacon.

"All that has to be done is to open up both their graves and see which one turned over last Friday night."

Billy was up the creek

Billy had been warned to be on his best behaviour when his wealthy aunt arrived for a brief holiday.

It was at tea during the first day of her stay that Billy kept staring at her. Then, when the meal was almost finished, he said: "Auntie, when are you going to do your trick?"

"What trick is that, dear?" she inquired.

"Well," replied Billy, "Dad says you can drink like a fish."

Broom bother

The village roadman seemed to be having a spot of trouble as the vicar cycled past. It looked as if the broom handle had come away from the head.

On his return about two hours later, the vicar was surprised to see him still struggling. He got off his bike and asked what the difficulty might be. "Well, ole bewty, thass like this here," said the roadman. "I hev put the duzzy handle on twice. . . an' now the hid hev cum orff!"

Old manicurists never die — they've got life nailed.

OWLES HALL

These lines were composed during our two-week family stay at Owles Hall in Frostenden. In August, 1995, we exchanged homes with David and Shirley Woodward and their friend Jo. They arrived in crowded Cromer on the eve of Carnival Week. We arrived in rural Suffolk a few miles beyond Beccles as the hot summer continued along with the corn harvest. We had visited Owles Hall several times and made our affections clear. Now we were resident for a fortnight .....

Borrow a home, borrow a memory
Of sunlit stubble and freedom.

Dedicated to the Owles Hall regulars, David, Shirley and Jo.
From The Squatting Skippers ...
Keith, Diane, Danny and Robin, August, 1995

They are me and I am them —
Boys' shouts cover all years —
As a thin-skinned morning calls
And the branches murmur welcome

We are here and you are here —
Friends' smiles grace all Edens —
As a timeless summer drifts
And the pigeons coo-coo loudly

It is now and it is then —
Folks' needs light all lanes —
As a moorhen dashes past
To mock the need for slowness

We are gone and you are home —
Fields' smiles a well-done brown —
 As an autumn chill advances
And puts a coat on pleasures

Museum of the Broads,
Poor's Staithe,
Stalham,
Norwich NR12 9DA.

'MARDLES AND MONOLOGUES AT THE MUSEUM'

KEITH SKIPPER AND FRIENDS

Present an atmospheric evening of
Broadland stories and legends, poems
and readings.
Also featuring a tribute to Allan
Smethust 'The Singing Postman'

Friday 6th April 2001 at 7:30pm
Tickets £6.00.
To book: enquire at the Museum or
Telephone: The Museum 01692 581681
Enid Baker 01692 670164
Di Cornell 01692 670754

Sponsored by Norvic Gas and
Lathams of Potter Heigham

Old nudists never die – they just couldn't bare it.

Baskets galore for another bumper catch at Great Yarmouth when herring was king.

"Feed the birds", you could hear Nelson cry
As overhead, sea-gulls flew by
Then one gull gave a swoop
Did an extra big 'poop'
Thass how Lord Nelson lost his left eye

Old taxmen never die — they keep coming back for more

Truth plain to see

A minister new to Norfolk decided a visual demonstration would brighten up his sermon.

So he placed four worms into four separate jars.

The first worm went into a container of alcohol.

The second worm was dropped into a container of cigarette smoke.

The third worm was placed into a container of chocolate syrup.

The fourth worm went into a container of good clean Norfolk soil.

At the end of his sermon, the minister reported the following results:

First worm in alcohol - dead.

Second worm in cigarette smoke — dead.

Third worm in chocolate syrup — dead.

Fourth worm in good clean soil — alive!

So the minister asked his congregation: "Now, what did you learn from this little demonstration?"

There was a long silence. Then one old boy at the back put up his hand and said: "Wuh, as long as yew drink, smoke an' eat chocolate, yew wunt hev wams!"

A few words of advice

Sarah was in a hurry and bustled past someone she knew without even giving the time of day.

On her return a few minutes later, the chap she had ignored called out to her: "Well, yew might ha'spoke even if yew sed nuffin."

Old dairymaids never die — they just churn to butter.

An early Press Gang get-together for a show at Sheringham Little Theatre.

Another outing with All Preachers Great and Small. My ecclesiastical chums (left to right) are Brian Patrick, David Woodward and Ian Prettyman.

NORFOLK

Alone, with your beauty kissed by the sea,
Remote, but so fair.
Beckoning no one, welcoming few
Your secrets to share.
Jealously guarding all that is yours
Naturally shy.
So much to offer, yet wanting to hide
From inquisitive eye.
Aware, always watching the world outside
Your vigil begun.
Trusting? Not progress,
Making no sound,
Lest predator come.

Cherry Burnage (Longham)

The Salthouse view (Trevor Allen).

Proud family day at Buckingham Palace in 2007 as Skip collects his MBE (My Bewtiful Embellishment).

NORFOLK SEEN FROM THE WELSH MOUNTAINS

Only a Welshman can really appreciate Norfolk.
Norfolk is Wales in reverse.
It points the other way, the cold flat levels of Europe
instead of the soft wet heights of Ireland.
Its mountains are all under the surface,
Its riches above it.
The openness of Norfolk is the absence of Welsh mountains.
You have to have grown up with gradients all around you to know this.
The big skies are the big open sigh of non-valleys,
the freedom from Welsh impediments.
Instead of grey cloud-capped mountains closing you in —
that great North Sea lapping you out.
Instead of a blood-misted history of towering defiance in defeat
generations of stubborn invaders placidly seduced.
Instead of the sunset West haunted with legends of greatness past,
the level sun rising in the East forever new.
Instead of Arthur the sleeping hero-king, Hereward the Wake.
Instead of the furious vowels, the clucking deprecatory consonants.
Welshman rant with glorious indignation
but always give in in the end.
Norfolkians smile sideways and don't argue
But never do what they're told either.
Welshmen rhapsodize about the freedom and calm and the endless
    horizons.
Norfolkians take it for granted.

Gareth Calway

SIZZLING SURVEY

Tourist boards tend to deliver statistics by the charabanc load.

Billions of pounds, millions of visitors, thousands of jobs. Figures are so big it's hard to argue with them. But that must mean they'll never know when we've reached saturation point.

In the interest of fairness and balance, qualities attracting so many to Norfolk to discover holiday routes or to put down full-time roots, I conducted a completely impartial survey on and around Cromer's bustling streets and seafront just as the summer season's peak approached.

I couldn't reach as many locals as I would have liked as 76 per cent prefer to stay out of sight until October. A few visitors claimed they couldn't understand what I was on about. Still, here's what tourism can mean to Cromer on one hot afternoon in late July:

Average journey by car through town centre provided 998 drivers with perfect chance to catch up with holiday reading.

Of these drivers, 66 also found time to pop out and buy new books along the way — and 15 joined the local library service.

A total of 1795 pedestrians struck up friendships while waiting to cross the road. On one especially busy corner, there were nine reunions, four proposals of marriage, three trial separations, two natural births and one irretrievable breakdown.

Out of 30 local businesses questioned, all agreed there were plenty of people about. But shops were invariably suffering from a common Norfolk affliction ... "They ent spendin' noffin'"

Of 688 visitors carrying fish and chips, 98 per cent preferred eating them outside, seats overlooking promenade and pier a favourite spot. Nearly 700 plump seagulls and starlings said they approved of tourism in general.

Just under 82 per cent of visitors on the seafront said they felt obliged to try Cromer Crabs during their stay. "You wouldn't leave Heacham without a sprig of lavender, Great Yarmouth without candyfloss or Sidestrand without a poppy" proclaimed a woman from Derby.

The Cromer Pier refurbishment programme was applauded by all but two of 1584 people interviewed. One complained he couldn't get a signal on his mobile phone. The other complained that he could — and he'd come on holiday from Aberdeen for "a wee bit o'free peace and quiet".

A cynical 17 per cent refused to take part, saying it was possible to twist replies to suit any cause.

A doff of the hat for one of Norfolk's top temples of culture, the Pavilion Theatre at the end of Cromer Pier.

GREEN GREW THE RUSHES

Green grew the rushes — standing like kings
Silver the water, the dragonflies' wings,
Away ran the fields to the cotton cloud skies,
And lark-rise at morning was sheer paradise.

Straight runs the highway — lanes up and down,
White lines and cats eyes — names of the towns,
We can go flying from A on to B,
Glasgow to London for afternoon tea,
New filling station — offers galore,
New roadside café — who could ask more?
And yet I sigh for what I used to know,
Just how it was here not so long ago.

Bring in the concrete — round and around,
Straight from the works, now just lay it all down,
All of the timber from forty nine trees,
Cut up and squared into nice two by threes,
Real easy parking on the estate,
Super the market — open 'till late,
Pile up the trolley as high as can be,
Where once the summer leaves danced merrily.

Coach in from London — cabs waiting there,
Take off like worker bees — go anywhere,
North side or south side — east side or west,
Tip for the cabby and wish him the best,
Here I remember I ran, as a child,
Sharing the secrets of things of the wild,
Gone now the hedges, white with the 'May',
Just for some shops and a new 'take away'.

Green grew the rushes — standing like kings,
Silver the water, the dragonflies' wings,
Away ran the fields to the cotton cloud skies,
And lark-rise at morning was sheer paradise.

Tony Palmer

Norwich's Castle Mall development in the 1980s inspired this hard-hat exercise on a bike (Alan Howard)..

Old fish and chips folk never die — they just get batter.

Wee problem

During the last war, some young lads from London were evacuated to a Norfolk farm. The farmer promised to take them to market by horse and cart.

They waited excitedly for this new form of transport. Suddenly one little boy ran into the house shouting: "Come quick, mister – the 'orse is losing 'is petrol!"

Diplomatic vacuity from a master

A government minister was touring rural Norfolk in a car. He got lost and stopped to ask an ancient local: "Where am I?"

"Yew're in that car," replied the rustic sage.

The politician smiled: "A perfect answer to a Parliamentary question. Short, true – and it doesn't add one iota to what we know already."

Silence is golden

A man went to the police station demanding to speak with the burglar who had broken into his home the previous night.

"You'll get your chance in court," said the desk sergeant.

"No, you don't understand," replied the man.

"I want to know how he got into the house in the middle of the night without waking my wife.

"I've been trying to do that for years!"

The insanity here is only temporary

A young female tourist from London, dressed in her summer finery, approached a Norfolk fisherman near the beach as he laid out his nets.

Her attempts at conversation were greeted with an occasional grunt. Finally, she shook her head and exclaimed, rather haughtily: "Norfolk is full of peculiar people." The fisherman looked up from his work and replied gently: "Yis, my bewty, but moost on'em hev gorn by October."

Old publicans never die – they just join the spirits.

East Ruston blacksmith's shop in the mid-1920s.

More hard work piling up for man and horse along the sugar-beet trail (Clifford Temple)

A reflection from a time gone by on the Norfolk Broads

Just taking stock

One of my favourite lines collected on Norfolk social rounds in recent years emerged from the winner's enclosure after a Mr Lovely Legs contest at Langham Street Fayre.

Philip Massingham, a sprightly 83-year-old local, fought off stiff rivals from all over the country to land the coveted title.

Probing for the secret of his success, I asked what he did before retirement. "I wuz a stockman" he replied … "an' thass why I hev got such good calves!

Doctor Richard Highmoor and his wife on their Litcham rounds a few years before the National Health Service arrived. (Litcham Historical Society).

Old ghosts never die — they just keep on coming back for exorcise

Market Street in Hingham waiting for a few signs of life.

Lessingham gets used to its own company.

Anglers try their luck at the Weir Pool in Buxton Lammas.

Old thieves never die — they only steal away.

Collecting thoughts

A young clergyman, fresh out of training, thought it might help him better understand the fears and temptations his future congregations faced if he first took a job as a policeman for a few months.

He passed the physical examination. Then came the oral exam to test his ability to act quickly and wisely in an emergency.

Among others questions he was asked: "What would you do to disperse a frenzied crowd?"

He thought for a moment and then replied: "I would pass round a collection plate."

He got the job.

A dignitary highly decorated

A proposal to put up a statue to an unpopular local dignitary was opposed by the town council – with one exception.

Horry argued that it would afford shelter in bad weather and shade in summer. And the pigeons would undoubtedly express the general feelings of the population in a most appropriate way.

Marmalade too pricey for Ma

The little girl's mother was by no means a prompt payer, so the grocer was far from polite when she asked about the price of marmalade. "Shillin' a jar," he said brusquely.

"Mum say she kin git it at Brown's for 11 pence."
"Then why dunt she git it at Brown's?"
"Cors they hent got enny."
"Well, I sell it fer 10 pence when I hent got enny."

Old gardeners never die — they merely go to seed.

Thornham, on the way to Hunstanton, clears the decks for a school rush.

A couple of youngsters stop to take in the beauties of Burnham Overy.

The parish church lords over all in Southrepps.

Old nostalgia buffs never die — they just keep living in the past.

Ideal bait

"How many fish have you caught?" asked the stranger as old George sat fishing on the bank.

"Well," said the old boy thoughtfully, "If I catch this one I'm arter, an' then tew more — I'll hev three!"

Train of thought

Billy and his wife were getting on an excursion train bound for Great Yarmouth at Ellingham station when they were told they wouldn't have to change at Beccles as usual.

"They're gorn ter hitch this here train to th'uther one" explained the porter.

Sure enough, at Beccles the Waveney Valley carriages were shunted on to the rear of the Yarmouth train. Only thing was this meant that those facing the engine were now sitting back to the engine.

"Thass a'rummin "said Billy. "I hev bin a'sittin' oppersite yew … an' now yew're sittin' oppersite ter me …… "

Just not fare

A rather posh woman got on a bus in Trunch and handed over a ten pound note.

"Oh dear, I don't seem to have a fifty pence for the fare" she said.

"Dunt yew fret, ole bewty" said the driver, "In a minnit yew'll hev 19 o'the beggars!"

Any way the wind blows

A motorist, taking a short cut through country lanes in Norfolk, came to a main road and found a signpost to Norwich. It was pointing in the opposite direction to the one he had expected.

An old man, clearly a local, wandered towards him.

He said: "Dunt yew tearke enny notice o'that ole pust – thass loose. When the wind's in the east, Norwich lay over there. When thass in the west, Norwich lay over here. . ."

Chance at last

Old George's wife had died and he called in the undertaker who asked when the funeral would take place.

"I should like ter bury the poor ole gal termorrer week" said George.

"Tomorrow week?" exclaimed the undertaker. "That means a lapse of eight days. Any special reason for that?"

"Well, thass like this here, marster" said George. "We're bin a'married for 65 year and we allus reckoned when we wuz a'cortin that if ever we git married we'd hev a quiet week on our own.

"This is only chance I're had — an' so now I'm gorter hev it."

Trying to bury their differences

An elderly Norfolk couple had led a cat-and-dog existence and hadn't spoken to each other for years. The husband fell ill and lay dying. His wife, anxious for a reconciliation before it was too late, decided to make the first move. She went upstairs to the old man's bedside and, breaking the long silence between them, whispered: "George, where dew yew want ter be buried?"

The answer came back without hesitation and in a rasping voice full of malice: "On top o' yew!"

Prize remarks

This one has whiskers on it — but remains a firm favourite wherever Norfolk tales are exchanged.

Harry won a goat in a raffle at the local horticultural show. A few weeks later his mate Charlie paid a call and asked how the goat was getting on.

"He's gittin' on orryte" said Harry, rather mysteriously.

"Well, where hev yew put 'im?" asked Charlie.

"I're got 'im in along wi' my missus in the bedroom."

"Cor, blarst me!" exclaimed Charlie. "What abowt the smell?"

"Tell yer the trewth "said Harry, "th'ole goat dunt fare ter mind that a mite!"

Gentle stroll along Beach Road at Heacham with plenty of shady spots.

Special offer

"How much are them melons?" Ben asked the greengrocer.

"Seventy-five pence each or two for a pound"

"Right yew are" said Ben. "Here's 25 pence. I'll hev th'uther one."

PULHAM MARKET.

Pulham Market jogs along without much fuss.

Generous sort

An old Norfolk countryman went into a chemist's shop on market day and ordered a large bottle of sleeping pills.

"Let me hev the biggest yew're got …. Dunno what I'd dew wi'owt 'em" he confided. "I'd never git a night's rest, thass for sure."

The girl behind the counter warned him not to take too many at once. The old boy replied: "Cor, blarst, I dunt tearke 'em atorl — I gi' them to my ole gal."

Old football referees never die — they simply blow for extra time.

Age-old complaint

Horry went to see the doctor with knee trouble.

After a thorough examination the doctor said he thought the pain in the right knee was simply down to old age.

"I sharnt hev that" said Horry. "Both my knees are the same age — an' th'uther one's orryte!"

Just too late

"What a pretty little village!" enthused the woman tourist to her husband. "Let's go and ask that dear ole chap over there all about it. He must be an absolute fount of knowledge."

The old boy was sitting outside the pub minding his own business. "Would you happen to be the oldest inhabitant of this charming settlement?" he woman.

"Blarst, no" came the reply. "He went an' died larst week."

Heading for school at Syderstone, near Fakenham, with no obstacles in the way.

An unobstructed view along Oxburgh Road at Stoke Ferry.

Safe and sound

An old Norfolk woman was asked if she was nervous during the first world war when the Zeppelins came over. "Why, no, m'dear," she replied. "I knew the door wuz locked."

Moved to tears

A conscientious Norfolk father ceased chastising his son.

"Now, my boy, yew tell me why I hev punished yew." The boy went on crying.

"Thass it," he blubbered. "Fust yew pound the life owter me, an' then yew dunt know why yew've dunnit for!"

Puzzled by pasties

The village church choir went on its annual outing to the Norfolk seaside. The new young vicar, thinking it would be a treat, ordered oyster pasties for high tea instead of the usual fish and chips.

Old Henry, who had never seen such things before, gazed at them for a minute or two. Then he carefully took the top off one on his plate and peered inside suspiciously.

After poking it with his fork, he called: "Hi, parson, dew yew cum here a minnit. Suffin's died in my bun."

Old traffic wardens never die — they think life's just the ticket.

Food for thought

Sid's missus was bemoaning the fact she hadn't worn any new clothes for years.

"Any stranger cummin' here ter the house would tearke me for the cook, not the owner!"

Sid looked up from his newspaper: "Nut if they stayed fer dinner, they wunt!

Shopping interests to the fore at Martham, near Great Yarmouth, when a quiet stroll and a few pence went a long way.

Good old daze

Grandma was telling off one of her grandsons.

"Trubble wi' youngsters terday is they hev tew much money ter spend. We had ter work long an' hard when I wuz young and there wunt no time fer skylarkin' abowt. Dew yew know what your grandfather wuz gittin' when he married me?"

"No," said the young 'un, "an' I bet he dint neither!"

Poor pussy

Billy came home from work to find his young wife in tears.

"Oh, William!" she sobbed, "The first meat pie I ever baked for you and the cat got it."

"Dunt yew, fret my bewty" he consoled her. "I'll get yew anuther cat termorrer."

VILLAGE GREEN, WOODBASTWICK.

The village green at Woodbastwick, eight miles from Norwich and still basking in its rural flavour.

Photo bargain

Gal Nelly came from the photographic studio. She showed Horry the result.

"That dew mearke me look a lot older than what I am" she said.

"Thass orryte," replied Horry. "That'll searve yew th'expense of hevin' 'nuther one took learter on."

Tucking in

"Another bite like that, young woman, and yew'll hatter leave this tearble" scolded a Norfolk mother.

"Another bite like that an' I'll be finished!" said the dear little mawther.

DERSINGHAM VILLAGE.

Dersingham — another village relishing an age before traffic.

A vicar's wife has to think fast

The vicar's wife peered out of the window and saw a familiar figure coming up the garden path.

SKIP'S WINNER

If all the people who sleep in church were laid end-to-end, they'd be a lot more comfortable.

She called to her husband: "William, here comes that dreadful bore Mrs Claypole. I suppose she's here to discuss the most recent sins of our parishioners. You'd better disappear to your study upstairs."

The vicar did so.

After nearly an hour of listening and nodding, his wife excused herself, went to let the cat out and took it to the kitchen for a saucer of milk. William, noting the end of conversation and hearing the coast was clear. He called out over the banister: "I'll be down in a minute, dear, now that dreadful bore has gone."

Unflustered, his wife, in sweet dulcet tones, called up the stairs: "Oh, but you must come down at once, William. That dreadful bore went over an hour ago. Mrs Claypole is here now."

Old taxi drivers never die — they just take the long way round

The Norfolk nerve centre where Skip proves he doesn't live entirely in the past (Rose Siggee).

Deathly hush

"Do you believe in life after death?" the company boss asked one of his young employees.

"Yes, sir" came the confident reply.

"That's good," said the boss, "because after you left early yesterday to go to your grandmother's funeral, she called in to see you."

Old reporters never die — they simply meet the deadline.

Lightning Source UK Ltd.
Milton Keynes UK
UKOW04f2221211115

263247UK00002B/42/P